ECO-ADVENTURES

ECO-ADVENTURES

Exploring the World's Natural Wonders

TRISTAN EVERGREEN

QuillQuest Publishers

CONTENTS

CHAPTER 1

Introduction

The introductory chapter provides an overview of eco-adventures and their importance to the environment. Eco-adventures are termed as "purposeful journeys that use the strength of nature to rejuvenate self and society". What differentiates eco-tourism from travel is that it includes a consciousness for the environment and cultural well-being of destinations. There is an emphasis on improving personal health and outlook through bettering the world. Defined by ATTA (Adventure Travel Trade Association) and the Nature Conservancy, eco-tourism is a responsible way of travel to natural areas that conserves the environment and sustains the well-being of local people/ecosystems. Countries that are home to natural wonders are often unsuitable for large-scale development. This raises a problem when trying to conserve natural territories. Eco-tourism allows for conservation through preservation. In a study done in Hawaii, tourists participating in eco-tourism activities spent more money per trip, stayed longer, and used more accommodations than regular sun and sea tourists. Step by step, tourists are making an effort to travel with a purpose and ideal for the environment, so surely it is possible to maintain touristic revenues through eco-tourism, in turn providing an economic incentive for conservation. Evidently, eco-tourism provides a way to devalue lands and make it more profitable to keep them as natural reserves.

CHAPTER 2

Benefits of Eco-Adventures

National parks and eco-adventure tourism have a close relationship, even though less energy and resources have been dedicated to understanding the actual needs of ecotourism in other settings. Eco-adventure explorers, trekkers, and rafters are seriously concerned with the preparation and management policies that restrict the type and degree of human influence. The history of national parks has shown a continuum of changing concepts and evolutions. Emerging new ideas and management policies for wilderness parks and renewable resources areas have posed a diversity of conflicting viewpoints and values. Practitioners of eco-adventure tourism share a vision with the current conservation movement, to maintain the earth's wildland.

Environmental conservation is a tremendously well-known rationale for eco-adventure journey, outdoor sporting events, and tourist-oriented trips into natural areas. Eco-adventure tourism is growing on such a scale in most countries that not enough scientific and educational research has been conducted on how to maintain the integrity of the natural world and capitalize on the benefits that tourism can convey to the maintenance of natural resources. Eco-adventure tourism is a nature primarily based largely form of tourism in which tourists seek and engage with relatively untouched areas away from urban settings, often seen as the empty white sand beach and clear ocean, rivers that weave through deep valleys, and famous spots that provide increased opportunities for viewing wildlife. It is travel to destinations where the flora, fauna, and cultural heritage are the primary attractions.

CHAPTER 3

Planning an Eco-Adventure Trip

The first thing to consider before planning your trip is what type of destination you want to go to. Different types of eco-adventures are catered for in different types of places. Do you want to explore the rainforest, the desert, the mountains, an island, or a remote village? Do you want to go somewhere remote, or are you looking for somewhere closer to a main town or city? Different people have different things in mind for an eco-adventure. Some may want to get away from all signs of modern society, whereas others may feel more comfortable in doing so. Choose the destination that suits your preference. Eco-adventure trips are usually into remote areas, so if you are going to a remote area, be sure to learn about the culture and language of the area. Knowing some of the language and cultural differences may save you from any inconveniences, and it helps to show respect to the local community. From here, you can gain a pretty good idea of the destination as to where you want to go.

Don't just head off to the airport and go to the first place you think of. To maximize your eco-adventure experience, planning is essential. From your choice of destination to the length of your trip, spending time planning your trip before you leave helps make your trip more enjoyable and helps you be prepared for any downfalls. With a positive outcome, this will give you more knowledge and experience for future eco-adventures!

CHAPTER 4

Eco-Adventures in North America

For travelers who prefer rugged mountains and forests to coral reefs and banana daiquiris, eco-adventure travel in North America offers endless opportunities. Hiking or backcountry skiing in North America's varied mountain ranges has its own particular excitement. In the lower 48 states, the Colorado Rockies, the Sierra Nevada of California, the Cascades of the Pacific Northwest, and the White Mountains of New Hampshire all offer good backcountry experiences. Venturing further north into Canada, the wilderness trails become even more extensive, including the famous Chilkoot Trail in the Yukon, which leads from Alaska to the Klondike. East and west from the trail, a vast system of even more remote trails can take hikers to places few people ever visit. Quebec, with its unique culture and beautiful mountain wilderness, is another popular destination for North American wilderness adventure travel. And ultimately, Canada's arctic wilderness can offer the ultimate in remote travel, to those with the experience and determination to undertake it.

CHAPTER 5

Eco-Adventures in South America

Venezuela: The Gran Sabana is a region of unique beauty and landscape. Here, Venezuela's highest waterfall, Angel Falls, drops from the top of a "tepui" (table-top mountain). The Roraima trek follows a route used by Sir Walter Raleigh in his search for El Dorado. The route climbs gradually through regions rich in wildlife and passes through Pemon Indian communities. The destination, El Roraima, is a tepui with a summit large enough to be a small island. The area is on the Venezuela/Brazil/Guyana frontier. Tepuis are quartzite table mountains found in the Guiana Highlands of South America, especially in Venezuela and western Guyana. These mountains are of ancient origin and the flat top of the tepuis is often covered by dense cloud forest. The isolation of the plateaus has led to a great deal of endemism, and the tepuis are unique in the biogeography of South America.

Intro: South America is a paradise for nature lovers. The widespread Amazon rainforest is home to an incredibly diverse range of flora and fauna, and is also inhabited by several indigenous tribes. The Andes, the world's longest mountain range, extends from Venezuela to Chile. With its multitude of attractions, opportunities for eco-adventures are plentiful in South America.

CHAPTER 6

Eco-Adventures in Europe

The best place for wolf tracking is in Slovakia with a local wildlife expert. Even if you are unsuccessful in seeing wolves, the experience of being in the wilderness at night is unforgettable. You will almost certainly hear wolves calling, and the Carpathians are the best place in Europe for seeing and hearing bears. Brown bears are relatively common in many areas, but the best place to see them is in the mountains on the Romanian border. Several companies offer bear watching trips with an overnight stay in a hide."

The Carpathians are one of the few mountain areas in Europe that are relatively untouched by man. They are sometimes referred to as the Green Pearl of Central Europe.

"What is it about Europe that attracts so many tourists? For some, it is the art and culture, while for others, it is the history. For nature lovers, the attraction is the diversity of landscapes and wildlife. There are eco-adventure opportunities to suit all tastes, from walking in coastal nature reserves to wolf tracking in the Carpathian mountains.

CHAPTER 7

Eco-Adventures in Africa

Specific eco ventures offer the chance to get up close to some of Africa's most famous yet threatened wildlife. This could be tracking gorillas in Uganda, witnessing the wildebeest migration in Kenya, or seeing the Big 5 in South Africa. Such experiences can have an educational slant, and those involved will be able to gain an understanding of some of the unique animals and their habitat. Usually, visitors will be encouraged to stay in lodges near the wildlife sites. These are often specifically designed to have as little impact on the environment as possible and can offer a very tranquil and secluded experience.

The best places to visit in search of eco-adventure are areas where there are large national parks or reserves. Countries whose infrastructure and political ambiguity have led to depleted tourism often have the best areas, as they can be off the beaten track for general tourists and offer a more surreal experience. Unfortunately, often the logistics of getting to some areas can be quite difficult and frustrating.

Encompassing the vast and contrasting landscapes of the deserts, savannahs, and rainforests, Africa offers a prime opportunity for eco-adventure. The continent supports a diverse range of ecosystems and is teeming with varied wildlife. There is a fragile balance between animals and the environment, and travelers can witness some spectacular sights and sounds of wild Africa. Eco ventures are numerous, varying from national parks to specific wildlife experiences.

CHAPTER 8

Eco-Adventures in Asia

In Southeast Asia, forests are gold. The area is covered by rainforest, considered the oldest ecosystem on earth, and dominated by tropical evergreen and deciduous trees. First-timers to all this green will undoubtedly start in Borneo, one of the few places relatively untouched by the modern age. Bank is covered by an umbrella of trees, an undergrowth of shrubs, plants apartment of leeches and water-carriers and supported by a staggering 15,000 different species of flowering plants. It's enough to make a botanist kick off his hiking boots and write poetry. This natural heritage has not gone unnoticed by the Irish. Alan Watson, a PADI course director and diving instructor of 12 years, said that it was the diving, not just the culture, which originally attracted him to Thailand. "I'm still not bored with the diving here. There's amazing marine life in the area," he explained. He returns at least once or twice a year to instruct diving and even brings Irish students on an annual diving trip to the Similan Islands.

CHAPTER 9

Eco-Adventures in Oceania

This chapter should leave any lover of the environment astounded and enthusiastic about the prospect of travel through the South Pacific. The combined images and education offered provide a real incentive for those wishing to understand a culture and environment beyond the reaches of conventional tourism.

Costin has divided the South Pacific into three sections. Melanesia: Described as the 'dark islands,' is comprised of New Guinea and islands of the Pacific including Vanuatu, New Caledonia, Fiji, and the Solomon Islands. The Micronesian Islands include the Northern Mariana Islands, Guam, Wake Island, Palau, the Marshall Islands, Kiribati, and Nauru. The land of Polynesia is a large triangle including Hawaii, Easter Island, and New Zealand. With his firsthand recollections of traveling, Costin accurately depicts the islands' natural settings and rich cultures, offering original with a classic feel of Polynesian music and dance.

Eco-Adventures in Oceania provides a solid introduction to the natural wonders waiting to be explored in the South Pacific. Here, Costin describes the wide variety of eco-tourism opportunities available in this stunningly beautiful region, filled with a truly unique mixture of dense rainforests, precious coastline, and tiny tropical islands. This chapter acts as a basic guide for anyone wishing to travel through Oceania, providing a taste of the ecologically rich and diverse landscapes which make this region so special.

CHAPTER 10

Eco-Adventures in Antarctica

An eco-adventure trip to Antarctica is a glimpse of the world as it once was. The great frozen continent is the final frontier on Earth for wildlife and those who wish to view it. Antarctica's pristine environment is exemplified by the Biological Monitoring and the Long-Term Ecological Research sites on Signy Island. These research projects allow visitors to view the diverse wildlife and how they are linked by marine and polar environments. From killer whales to petrels, the sites provide a banquet of wildlife set against a breathtaking glacial backdrop. The various ecotourism operators provide numerous cruises and land trips to view such majestic sites, and they are linked with the local research stations to provide the best environmental interpretation possible to visitors. The chance to view true wilderness is what lures many eco-tourists to the frozen south, and the continent boasts some of the most dramatic landscapes found on the planet. Whether it's an iceberg-studded bay, a glacier calving, or the haunting isolation of the polar plateau, there is something to captivate every visitor. High visitor site or activity density levels can have detrimental impacts on Antarctic wildlife and the environment itself. To manage and mitigate these impacts, the International Association of Antarctica Tour Operators (IAATO) has adopted extensive measures to ensure that visitor activities are monitored and audited. Close coordination with Antarctic Treaty Parties and the Scientific Committee on Antarctic Research (SCAR) helps ensure that activities are consistent with environmental management goals for Antarctica, a continent dedicated to peace and science.

CHAPTER 11

Rainforest Exploration

Low agricultural prices and a rapidly increasing national population mean that colonization and subsequent deforestation and for the foreseeable future pose the greatest threat to the Amazon and its peoples. It is estimated that up to 33% of all Andean and Amazonian slopes will be permanently deforested if current colonization trends continue. The tourism industry has a role to play in offering a viable alternative that has less impact on the rainforest and provides a sustainable income for local people. One dollar generated from ecotourism can have the conservation impact of an area being logged to provide timber worth between $100 and $2,400. The choice is clear; the hardest part will be to steer the nascent ecotourism industry away from repeating the mistakes made with other industries in the past by ensuring its practices are sustainable.

The Amazon, the world's largest tropical rainforest, is replete with ecological wonders. It contains one out of ten known species on Earth, 40,000 plant species, 3,000 freshwater fish species, and more than 370 types of reptiles. The sheer volume of species here has led ecologists to refer to the Amazon as the "last biological frontier". The Cosñipata Valley, at the meeting point of Andes and Amazons, has one of the most varied and impressive bird lists of any single site in the world. Tambopata, near Puerto Maldonado, is home to an incredible diversity of butterflies. The Heath River, a tributary of the Madre de Dios, provides some of the most intact lowland macaw clay licks. Manu National Park, the world wildlife capital, can boast an incredible 1000 species of bird, 200 species of mammals, 200 species of reptiles, and 100 species of frog! Madre de Dios contains 10% of the world's known bird species, more than 2,000 species. These areas and their unique inhabitants are under constant threat from encroaching civilization, as people move out from the mountains and Andean highlands in search of a better standard of living. The government gives away great tracts of land to colonists, who try to eke out an existence by practicing unsustainable agriculture and logging.

CHAPTER 12

Mountain Trekking

On any continent, mountain trekking offers an unforgettable experience that begins the minute you start preparing for the trek. High-altitude travel is an acquired taste, and there are few places in the world that offer a more pristine and awe-inspiring environment than the high mountains on the major land masses. When one thinks of mountain trekking, one typically is referring to working their way up to 18,000 feet on the snow-covered peaks of the world. However, it is an activity that can be done at many different levels. From the Cordillera Blanca in Peru to the Alps in Europe, Africa's Mt. Kenya to the high peaks of the Karakorum and the Himalaya, to trekking in the Rocky Mountains of the United States, there are a wide array of choices of where to go mountain trekking. As a rule of thumb, however, it is best to start trekking at a relatively low altitude and gradually work your way higher over the days to follow in order to best acclimatize to the change in altitude. This itinerary is leading to a classic mountain climb of Island Peak in the Khumbu. Island Peak is a trekking peak, which means it is a peak that can be climbed by someone with little or no mountaineering experience. Usually, the term "trekking peak" is referring to a peak that is under 7,000 meters and is achievable with about 3-4 weeks of time off of work. Coming from sea level, an activity such as mountain trekking will lead to increased physical fitness and an overall feeling of good health. Going for a nice trek in the backcountry provides a little escape from the hustle and bustle of modern-day society. The natural environment and peacefulness of the mountains is something that cannot be matched and is therefore the reason why people keep coming back again and again for another mountain trek.

CHAPTER 13

Wildlife Safaris

Because wildlife is spread across the continents, ecotourists have taken a variety of approaches to seeing it. Some have followed migration routes of large mammals. This has spawned a massive nature travel industry in places like Kenya and Tanzania, where tourists are packed into minivans and carried around vast national parks. The practice is often criticized for rewarding corrupt governments and doing little to help local communities or the environment. On the other end of the spectrum are operations like the Tahuayo Lodge in the Peruvian Amazon. This is an ecotourism success story, where local people are in full control, tourism revenues go directly to conservation and community projects, and the wildlife, including animals that are rare or nonexistent in any national park in Amazonian countries, is abundant. E.O. Wilson has said that the Amazon forests of Peru are the place to see wildlife.

CHAPTER 14

Scuba Diving and Snorkeling

The activity/science of snorkeling can be a valuable tool to educate or train individuals in aquatic sciences, especially when field studies are not possible. During snorkelling, species documentation by simple methods such as photography or sketching can contribute valuable data to aquatic sciences. Because snorkelling is a simple activity, it is within the reach of most people regardless of age or fitness, not requiring a large financial or time input. Skills in snorkeling are easily mastered, or if forgotten are quickly picked up again. Although snorkeling is not without its uncomfortable aspects, a snorkeler need only endure cold, currents, poor visibility etc. So for these reasons and due to lower risks than diving, many individuals retain snorkeling as an activity well into old age.

Scuba diving and snorkelling are great ways to experience marine and freshwater environments. The natural curiosity present in divers and snorkelers is given direction through diving and snorkelling activities. This is because aquatic environments are alien to us, and progress in our understanding of them is typically through direct experience. Using simple observation, questions such as "what was that?" and "I wonder why this happens?" are readily answered. Through this questioning process, divers and snorkelers can develop an understanding of aquatic life and environments. For those interested in natural history and aquatic ecosystems, many simple questions may be a powerful motivator to try diving or snorkelling.

CHAPTER 15

Volcano Expeditions

Because of this, and the often remote locations of these natural wonders, volcanoes have become a focus for adventure tourism. As an activity that involves visiting fragile, pristine, and undisturbed natural areas, ecotourism has great potential to alter the environment and natural societies of the areas in which it occurs. This is particularly relevant to volcano tourism, which often takes place in developing countries. High visitor numbers have the potential to damage the environment, and there is often little regulation or consideration for the potential damage caused. It is with this in mind that some researchers have carried out studies on the effect of ecotourism on volcanic environments, and ways in which tourism can be maintained in a sustainable manner.

Volcanoes are an intrinsic part of the world's natural marvels; phenomena that are perpetually reshaping the landscape as they create it. As such, they provide a natural laboratory in which to study the earth's processes. However, it is their aesthetics and their sometimes fearsome nature that attract so many to visit them. From the resplendent vegetation and vibrant, moldable landscapes that can be found on dormant volcanic slopes, to the awe-inspiring and raw displays of power provided by lava flows, ash clouds, and pyroclastic activity, volcanoes have held explorers and visitors transfixed for centuries.

Remote, active, and inhospitable are words often used to describe some of the world's strangest terrain. It's not surprising, then, for those who have ventured into these unique landscapes, that it is often within or near the isolated areas surrounding active volcanoes. Around the world, countless numbers of volcanoes have built landscapes that are as intriguing as they are inhospitable, and some of the most spectacular locations for ecotourism involve hikes, climbs, or expeditions into these mysterious locales.

CHAPTER 16

Desert Adventures

For a guaranteed adventure in desert travel, one should consider crossing a desert by camel or by 4x4 vehicle. Rugged and remote regions such as the Kimberley in Western Australia or the deserts of Oman and Saudi Arabia provide ideal settings for such experiences. Time taken to plan and undertake a vehicle-based expedition through desert regions need not be a costly or time-consuming exercise. The preparatory planning stage is, in fact, half the fun, and some very rewarding trips can be achieved in a 1-2 week time frame.

Trekking through the 'thirsty' deserts of The Simpson, Sahara, or the Sinai and Arabian deserts can provide a modern-day traveler with an experience of the hardships endured by the people and cultures indigenous to those regions. In some cases, the traveler's experience may be somewhat softened in comparison! To take anything from a day hike to an extended trek into desert regions can be a fulfilling test of one's fitness and endurance. An orientation to the shifting sands and featureless landscapes of the world's great deserts can also prove to be an interesting and rewarding experience.

Names can be misleading. Adaptation is an accurate term for the skills and characteristics required to travel through arid and desolate places, rather than simply survival. What sounds like a daunting and somewhat uneventful experience can be anything but. Consider the varied landscapes desert cover; from shifting sand dunes, to rugged mountainous regions. The hardy and resilient people and cultures found in desert regions have developed many unique and interesting ways in which to live and travel.

CHAPTER 17

Canopy Tours and Ziplining

For variety and adventure in nature travel, Mindo is unequaled. Come and help preserve the beauty and diversity of this unique paradise.

For the more serious biology enthusiast, a trip to the Mindo Nambillo Cloud Forest Reserve is a must. This 2000 hectare reserve consists of some of the most biologically diverse cloud forest in the entire world. Guided tours can familiarize you with some of the forest's 170 species of trees and the 400 species of birds. But to a true daredevil, there could be no greater excitement than being suspended over these forests in a thin metal cable! High above the forest floor, five different ziplines extend over two kilometers and with heights of up to 150 meters. This exhilarating ride allows you to witness the true expanse of the reserve while gaining a bird's eye view of its flora and fauna. For serious thrills a canopy tour will give you a swinging tour through the treetops on a series of five pulley operated ziplines that travel between 20 platforms constructed high in the trees.

A walk outside of town will almost always turn into a bird watching expedition. Guides are available and easy to find: any of them can show you a side of Mindo that you would never find on your own. Drifting silently on a canoe through the early morning mist, you can sight hundreds of exotic tropical birds. Adventurous types may want to join an inner-tubing tour on Mindo's Rio Cinto. You float eight kilometers down the river, careening through white water and drift into the heart of the forest. A similar horseback trip is also available to La Cascada waterfalls.

Along the western edge of the Andes in Ecuador rolls the uplands city of Mindo. In recent years, this cloud-forest area has become a mecca for birdwatchers. Its avian diversity—more than 450 species—draws naturalists, too. But more traditional tourists have yet to discover Mindo. This means that the lodgings are moderately priced and the town retains its unspoiled character. A mere 64 km (40 miles) north-west of Quito, the tranquility of Mindo will make you feel that you have journeyed to another world.

CHAPTER 18

Caving and Spelunking

Caving is exploring wild or non-commercial caves. This can involve anything from easy walks and climbs in large chambers to technical, vertical descents of great depth. It is an activity that can be enjoyed by people of all ages and abilities. Wild caving is the only way to see the most natural and untouched caves, see rare speleothems, or see beautiful and intricate passageways. A caver can see much more value and significance in the underground environment. With some training or research, they can start to understand the geology and long process involved in forming these intricate underground environments.

There are thousands of caves in the U.S. alone and many more thousands worldwide. Visiting these underground wonders is an exciting and rewarding adventure. Caves can be formed in many types of rock, and various geological processes can create caves of many sizes, shapes, and depths. Many caves are rich in spectacular mineral formations called speleothems. These are stalactites (hanging from the ceiling), stalagmites (growing up from the floor), columns, flowstone, and other deposits. The colors and forms of these features are breathtaking, and they are still forming today, very slowly. This fact is an indication of the time scales involved in the creation of caves; geologic processes usually occur over millions of years. All the more reason to visit these unique environments—they are fragile and must be protected in order for future generations to be able to enjoy them.

Caves have fascinated humans as early as the beginning of our existence. They are mysterious places, naturally carved into the earth and usually very complex. Caves and their untouched, pristine environments are unique in the world. They offer stunning vistas unlike anywhere else and contain some of the last unexplored areas on the planet.

CHAPTER 19

Rafting and Kayaking

Some trips consist entirely or mostly of river travel and are best suited to the canoe or raft, the only mode of transport that is both mobile and does not damage the environment. These must be confined to rivers or streams that are big enough for the craft being used, and smooth water is preferable to fast, shallow sections, where the risk of grounding or swamping is too great. Rapids are classified by their technical difficulty, with class I being fast moving water and class VI being unrunnable, with severe likelihood of injury to paddlers or death. Careful inquiries should be made about the nature of any rapids on a proposed route and their suitability to the party's abilities, since the skill of the paddlers and water levels required for safe negotiation of rapids can vary greatly. Low snowmelt or dam released rivers may not be suitable for canoeing in late summer. Tier I of the international scale is a useful reference point for assessing the difficulty of navigation to less fluent speakers of English. The capacity of canoes for carrying heavy loads makes them suitable for longer trips, with descent of the Yukon river leading to a several week journey, while white water canoeing is a more arduous and hazardous activity, usually limited to shorter trips on rivers of up to 14 days. Inflatable and rigid inflatable boats of various sizes are the modern choice for white water expeditions, since they are safe to the ground and forgiving in nature, and their high loading capabilities render even relatively small craft suitable for up to class IV rivers. Kayaks are a more demanding and technical way of descending white water and are not usually considered suitable for long wilderness trips because of the difficulty in carrying large expedition loads.

CHAPTER 20

Hiking and Camping

Hiking is a popular eco-activity that is as simple or as complex as one chooses to make it. A family can take a gentle, introductory hike in the countryside, perhaps exploring the flora and fauna of the area by identifying species of wild plants and insects. This can be followed on another occasion by a more serious day-long attempt to climb a small mountain. A well-organised hiking trip can be a very low-impact holiday and it is an activity well suited to exploration of the wilderness and natural areas. With the minimum of gear, the hiker is self-sufficient and can utilise established trails and campsites or go off trail into more remote areas. Minimal impact bushwalking or hiking is a style of travel that is done with the least possible intrusion on the environment and the least possible harm to the local people. At its core is a philosophy which seeks to be ecologically friendly, technologically simple and often spiritually rewarding. It was the desire to go off trail, deeper into the wilderness and the experience gained from a number of expeditions in Australia and overseas that led to the formation of Hidden Trails. Ron and Kirsty Woolley have led hiking parties in remote areas for over 12 years and their passion is in exploring the last remaining pockets of wilderness and diverse natural areas. From coastal heath to rainforest and remote desert gorges, Australia has many unique environments which can only be truly appreciated on foot. This discovery of the natural environment is an essential component of an eco-holiday and hiking is one of the best ways to do it.

CHAPTER 21

Birdwatching and Nature Photography

Birdwatching and Nature Photography Birdwatching and photography are nature pursuits so close to ecotourism that they practically are ecotourism in and of themselves. Think of them as ecotourism focusing on birds or focusing on particular aspects of the grand mosaic of nature with the intent of capturing the moment for further reflection and enjoyment. The commitment needed for birdwatching is usually slight, but for some it becomes a strong interest lasting a lifetime. Time and patience are the essentials; the willingness to go and walk (or just sit) in natural areas in the absence of manmade noise and confusion. This in and of itself is a liberating experience. Birdwatching often leads to a general interest in natural history and an accumulation of information on a wide variety of plants, animals, and ecosystems, and an increased interest in conservation of these things. A simple pair of eyes or binoculars is the only essential equipment, although serious birdwatchers often end up with a selection of field guides and maybe a tape recorder or camera for documentation. Birdwatching trips and tours are now offered at many ecotourism destinations and watching birds is considered one of the more desirable special interests from the standpoint of the local peoples and their resources. Watching birds provides a treasure trove of memories for the ecotourist, and information collected on bird distribution and abundance can be useful to those concerned with conservation and management of natural areas. Capture on film is another useful source of data and photographs can be valuable educational tools.

Preface 1. Defining Ecotourism 2. History of Nondomesticated Natural Areas [...] 20. Hiking 21. Birdwatching and Nature Photography 22. Canoeing and Rafting 23. SCUBA and Snorkeling [...] 28. Ecotourism and the Nature of Ecotourists 29. Marketing Ecotourism 30. The Future of Ecotourism [...]

CHAPTER 22

Indigenous Cultural
Experiences

Visitors traveling with conservation organizations or in small groups can enrich their understanding of the complexities of tropical rainforests. They can learn about the lives of indigenous peoples who depend on these forests. The best way to learn about rainforest culture is through a village stay. Many organizations in countries like Belize, Costa Rica, Ecuador, and Peru can arrange for travelers to spend time in indigenous villages. This learning experience is truly mutual and transformative. During my ethnographic fieldwork in a small Kichwa community in Ecuador's Amazonian region, I was continually amazed at how much I learned each day—whether about medicinal plants, natural history, or sustainable farming practices. At the same time, villagers were keenly interested in the ways of the outside world and were often alarmed to hear about deforestation and cultural change in North America. Village stays foster deep respect and understanding and often lead to close, long-term friendships. Other travelers may not travel to these regions for the explicit purpose of studying rainforest culture but end up having rich cultural experiences all the same. During lowland South America's high ecotourist season, trails in national parks and other protected areas are often busy with groups of foreign birdwatchers. This is a windfall for local indigenous guides who possess uncanny abilities to spot rare birds and other wildlife and are often able to impart their intimate knowledge of the forest and its inhabitants. In a similar vein, indigenous artists and craftspeople can find new markets for their products among foreign tourists, who may be eager to learn about the cultural significance of these items. While such encounters can sometimes result in negative cultural and environmental impacts, they can also provide valuable—often eye-opening—insights for outsiders into indigenous knowledge and worldviews.

CHAPTER 23

Sustainable Tourism Practices

But it is travel and transportation that can be the most damaging part of tourism. A major part of sustainable tourism is to offset the damage done from travel through the protection and often restoration of the natural environment at the tourism destination. An alternative to this is the concept of EcoTransport; this is where a tourist travels on foot, bicycle, or other non-motorized transport in the belief that the journey is as much a part of the experience as the destination. EcoTourism New Zealand is trying to promote the concept of cycle touring in New Zealand due to the fact that the average tourist has more contact with locals and spends more money in the country than any other type of tourist. This is more sustainable as less money is used to promote the country overseas and the cost benefits are spread over many communities at grassroots level.

Sustainable tourism practices aim to lessen the adverse impact tourism spots have on the environment and maximize the positive contribution of tourism for local communities. Sustainable tourism, adventure travel, eco-tourism, and nature-based tourism are just a few of the terms used for achieving these goals. Sustainable tourism businesses are those that adopt principles and implement practices that make a real difference by following these practices. Low impact visitors are people who take nothing away and also give nothing, such as the respectful tourist. Long haul travelers sometimes give a little, such as constructed buildings or litter. If tourism is controlled properly, the net balance can still be positive.

CHAPTER 24

Conservation and Environmental Education

This theme has received increasing attention by some scholars who have identified a range of impacts from ecotourism. These range from indirect financial contributions to environmental advocacy by ecotourists to the damaging of the natural experience through over-commercialization. However, one of the most noted impacts that has the potential to do both harm and good is environmental education. This is perhaps the only conservation strategy where the potential is limitless. Educating visitors at the various abundant natural attractions has the potential to alter the attitudes and behavior of the public, to increase awareness and concern for the environment, and to promote public support for conservation. An increase in knowledge about the environment may change behavior leading to a more sustainable life-style. This may ultimately be the more effective way of dealing with the global environmental problems.

This is primary within the responsible tourism industry as one of the fastest developing forms of special interest tourism. The International Ecotourism Society defines ecotourism as responsible travel to natural areas that conserve the environment and improve the well-being of local people. Ecotourism has emerged out of the dramatic increase in nature-based tourism to some of the world's most pristine and remote regions.

41

CHAPTER 25

Eco-Lodges and Green Accommodations

While the term "eco-lodge" implies an environmentally friendly accommodation, many lodges are not sustainable nor are they involved in ecotourism. An eco-lodge should have the intention of conservation and education, but some accommodations use the term for marketing on a nature-based setting and wildlife viewing, while making no effort to run an environmentally friendly operation. This led TIES to develop a rating system for eco-lodges based on how sustainable and environmentally friendly the operation is. This system is designed to encourage lodges to adopt more earth-friendly practices. Becoming a TIES member and going through the rating system will give a lodge more credibility and incentive to become environmentally friendly.

Accommodations are a key aspect of travel, and numerous organizations are working to make this sector of the travel industry more environmentally friendly. Eco-lodges are nature-based, smaller-scaled, and in natural settings. This niche in the tourism industry has taken off since the 1980s. Eco-lodges seek to preserve pristine areas of the natural environment. Accommodations are built in a sustainable fashion and are often partially or fully powered by renewable energy. The use of local and natural building materials is common. Some eco-lodges are designed for bird watching, others to give visitors a close encounter with wildlife. There are eco-lodges designed for adventure travel, while others are geared towards relaxation. Typically an eco-lodge will have an educational and/or conservation program as part of its mission to promote local and global environmental awareness. The International Ecotourism Society (TIES) defines eco-lodges as "accommodations that are built in an environmentally friendly manner and designed to protect the natural environment." This definition provides a general idea, but the types and styles of eco-lodges can be very diverse. TIES is an organization with a mission to help develop ecotourism. They provide guidelines and educational materials to promote sustainable travel. TIES holds conferences and has networking and marketing tools for those involved in any aspect of ecotourism.

CHAPTER 26

Responsible Wildlife Tourism

If you are interested in viewing wild animals, here are a few things you can do to ensure that while you are observing animals, you are minimizing your impact on them and their environment. Never feed wild animals. Feeding wild animals can have a number of harmful effects on both the animals and the people who come to see them. When animals are fed, they lose their natural instinct to forage. They become dependent on people for food, they may lose their fear of humans, and they may become aggressive in order to get food. Foods that people feed to wildlife are often very harmful. For example, the most common cause of death in white-tailed deer is by people feeding them food that is harmful to them. Always try to view wildlife from a distance. Do not attempt to go close to or handle the animals. Animals that are approached too closely may be more easily caught by predators. They may abandon nests, feeding sites, or young. A female animal that is caring for young must spend more energy protecting its young, have less success in raising its young, or may abandon them. If animals change their normal behaviors in response to human activity, they may have less success at survival. Female animals with young and animals that are preparing for migration or hibernation are particularly vulnerable to human disturbance.

CHAPTER 27

Eco-Friendly Transportation Options

Of course, one of the most eco-friendly ways to travel is by foot. By walking through a national park or natural wonder, you can avoid any negative environmental impact and truly experience being part of the nature around you. This is a wonderful way to travel and a fantastic form of exercise, but it can be time-consuming and may not be feasible when traveling long distances. In cases like this, you can opt to travel by bike. Many places have bike rental shops and bike-friendly pathways that make this a convenient and environmentally sound way to travel. Some mountainous areas have restrictions on traveling by bike, so be sure to inquire about regulations beforehand. Another form of eco-friendly transportation is a pack trip, i.e. travel with a donkey or horse carrying your supplies from one place to the next. This can be a unique experience in and of itself. One more option that could be surprising to some is traveling by canoe or kayak. In areas with lakes or rivers as a main attraction, this is an interesting and peaceful way to travel and the most environmentally friendly water transportation available. Each one of these options fits into the theme of the book and thus has much to offer the eco-conscious traveler. In today's high-tech world, public transportation is often overlooked as a means of traveling between major tourist destinations. Traveling by bus or train is less stressful than dealing with car rentals, parking, and directions. It eliminates the need for a GPS system that guzzles 4 AA batteries a day and it reduces the number of rental cars on the road. Traveling by bus or train is often more scenic as well, since these routes tend to pass through areas untouched by major highways. Also, many travel and tourism organizations offer package deals that will save you money on transportation and lodging when you choose to use their services. This can be an all-inclusive sustainable travel package.

TIPS FOR MINIMIZING ENVIRONMENTAL IMPACT

While air travel is the most environmentally damaging form of travel, it is often not realistic to give it up for the eco-adventurer who wants to explore the far reaches of the globe. A return flight from Europe to Australasia can release as much as 5-10 tonnes of CO_2 per passenger. Atmospheric concentrations of CO_2 are the highest they have been for the last 650,000 years and continuing to rise, contributing to climate change. A quick and easy way to at least offset the damage your flight has caused is to calculate and donate money to an organization that is working on a sustainable energy or tree planting project. This will help to 'mop up' the CO_2 you have emitted and will contribute to reducing the chance of future climate change while providing sustainable development for the future.

Offset your carbon emissions

Take the time to learn a little about the place you are going to visit, understand the culture and customs, and the current environmental issues facing the area. By learning about the place, you will gain a greater understanding and appreciation for the place you will visit. This will enrich your experience by providing a greater insight into the place, its people, and the natural wonders. Understanding the current environmental issues will enable you to travel more sensitively and see how you can contribute positively to the places you visit.

Learn before you go

Before you head off on your eco-adventure, it is worth considering how you can reduce your impact on the places you are visiting. While it is nearly impossible to travel without having some impact on the place you are visiting, being mindful of your impact can make a big difference. The tips below are to help you be a more responsible traveler, reducing the negative impact your visit could have on the environment.

CHAPTER 28

Safety and Health Considerations

Some countries do not have the same health, safety, and hygiene standards that are present in Europe, Australia, New Zealand, Canada, and the United States. In this chapter, the phrase "electric socket" often refers instead to a live wire and a hole in the wall, and drinking water can be undependable. If you are a parent, it is a good idea to have your family visit a travel doctor to discuss traveling in developing countries. You can expect your children to have most of the recommended immunizations, including typhoid, rabies, Japanese encephalitis, diphtheria, tetanus, hepatitis A and B, and possibly malaria medication. It is totally up to you and your personal ethics about which immunizations you receive. If you are on the move with the intent of interacting with locals, you may feel better knowing that you cannot give the locals hepatitis or some other something equally as unpleasant. On the other hand, if you are a fitness fanatic who does not want to "miss a beat" and tends to participate in the local nightlife with other westerners, you may feel better having more serious and potentially detrimental diseases covered. Please note that if you are on an organized tour, your tour company may still require high health and safety standards and refuse a full adventure itinerary. Be aware of this when booking flights and discussing travel plans with travel doctors and travel insurance companies.

CHAPTER 29

Packing Essentials for Eco-Adventures

Some items might seem like common sense, but people forget them. Since most eco-destinations are in developing, tropical countries, items such as mosquito repellent, sunscreen, lightweight waterproof pants and jacket are essential. Remember to pack only essential items, most eco-destinations do not have baggage handling and you may regret overpacking when you have to carry your bag 15 km to the accommodations. Buy or make a first aid kit. A small container of basic first aid items may come in handy. 1. A few adhesive bandages 2. Roll of gauze and small adhesive tape 3. Antiseptic in single-use packages 4. A few ibuprofen and acetaminophen 5. Any prescription medications you need. Remember to pack for the specific environmental and issues. Writing utensils, paper, books, and a camera are often useful for research or personal pleasure. While many destinations have potable water, water purification tablets can be quite useful. This is a multi-use item that can make a big difference for a person or a group doing an eco-tour. People with allergies should consider items such as a dust-mite proof pillowcase or a specific air filter mask. Finally, remember to pack all necessary travel documents. The sunk investment on a plane ticket will be completely wasted if one is denied entry at their destination. Visa regulations can differ greatly for each country, it is often wise to have a return ticket and proof of where you are staying while in the country. Also, make sure to have photocopies of all emergency contact numbers and relative information left at home. Now you are ready to travel to your eco-destination hindered with the smallest degree of impact on the environment and its people.

CHAPTER 30

Resources for
Eco-Adventure Travelers

Internet travel forums are a free and easy way for travelers to seek advice from other people who have similar traveling interests. Lonely Planet Thorn Tree is the most popular travel forum on the web, and it offers many suggestions for eco-tourists. Crafty travelers can often pick the brains of locals who are also forum members, and with a little luck can find a way off the beaten path without having to pay for an organized tour.

Eco-tour operators: One of the principal concerns for travelers is finding an eco-tour that is authentic. This is not always easy. Many mainstream tour operators add the term "eco" to attract more clientele, and often the tours are not any different from conventional ones. The International Ecotourism Society (TIES) offers some guidance for people looking for eco-friendly travel options, and they have a database of ecologically responsible tour operators. Although the Society has been criticized for being apologetic of some forms of eco-tourism that are not entirely beneficial to the environment, and its database is not completely definitive, it is still a useful tool for finding an authentic ecotour.

The efforts to conserve ecologically significant lands are directly tied to the dollars spent by the public to visit these areas; spending your travel dollars in a way that helps, not hinders the environment can make a big difference. Listed below are various resources travelers can use to ensure that their adventures are environmentally friendly.

CHAPTER 31

Conclusion

Eco-adventure travel is catching on very quickly and has made a substantial impact on tourism. While many travelers are now venturing out into the wilderness, there are still many who are unclear as to the difference between eco-tourism and other forms of nature-based travel. Hopefully, with this guide to the world's natural wonders, I have shed some light on both subjects and provided some helpful insights and tips to help others travel in a more responsible and culturally enhancing manner. Remember not to take the Earth's beauty for granted, for it is an ever-fleeting treasure that can be lost in an alarmingly short period of time. I encourage everyone to visit at least one of the many eco-destinations I have mentioned. By doing so, not only will you walk away with a greater understanding and appreciation of the world, but the money you have spent will greatly benefit the preservation and sustainability of that destination. It is an incredible way to help the environment and cultures of other nations, and a very rewarding experience for yourself.

What a journey it has been! I hope my writing has inspired the traveler in everyone to embark on their own eco-adventure. This conclusion is aimed at a gentle reminder of what has been discussed in this writing with a few encouragements for the reader to go out and discover some of the wonders of the world that I have mentioned. Offering a few final remarks about preserving the beauty of the Earth, and capturing the pure essence of other cultures, while trying not to sound too much like a politician.

9 798330 617937